Melt

Derick Burleson

Melt

Derick Burleson

MARICK PRESS

Library of Congress Cataloguing in Publication Data

Derick Burleson
Melt
Poetry. 1st Paperback Edition, 2011
ISBN 10: 1-934851-34-5
ISBN 13: 978-1-934851-34-0
Copyright © by Derick Burleson, 2011
Copyright © by Marick Press, 2011
Design and typesetting by Really Big Robot
Cover design by Really Big Robot
Cover art by Derick Burleson
Printed and bound in the United States

Marick Press
P.O. Box 36253
Grosse Pointe Farms
Michigan 48236
www.marickpress.com
Mariela Griffor, Publisher
Distributed by spdbooks.org
And Ingram

Marick Press is an independent literary press that publishes fine literature. Marick Press is a registered 501 (c) 3 non-profit organization and we rely on public and private funding to carry out the mission of publishing annually 6-8 titles in both hardcover and paperback covering a broad spectrum of topic that range from literary non-fiction, creative non-fiction, poetry, fiction and reprint of previously published titles.

Marick Press is not-for-profit literary publisher, founded to preserve the best work by poets around the world, including many under published women poets.

Marick Press seeks out and publishes the best new work from an eclectic range of aesthetics —work that is technically accomplished, distinctive in style, and thematically fresh.

ACKNOWLEDGMENTS

Were I to list here all the names of the people who have read this book, and who have offered their kind support, suggestions and friendship, that poem would be longer than this one. Thank you all.

I would also like to thank the editors of the following publications in which sections of *Melt* originally appeared, sometimes with different titles.

The Art of Angling (Alfred A. Knopf): [The fish itself was water made flesh] and [When the halibut gave themselves].

Cirque: [In the shadow I was breathing] and [I couldn't take it anymore].

New Orleans Review: [There is an order in the apparent chaos] and [Takes you at a gallop].

Of a Monstrous Child (Lost Horse Press): [There is an order in the apparent chaos], [Rain. What came pouring out], [An opening loosening relaxing], [Framed like this], [In the shadow I was breathing], [Sometimes I remember how you with], [Meanwhile the weather went from tropical to ice], [I'm kneeling before her devoting], [When she was gone my despair was a sea], [Pink essence of essence], [It was the rain coming into me], [It begins underground], and [I want to slide into you].

Poetry International: [The People came together at the farm], [My breath rose white into blue] and [Her nipples spoke to me only to me].

Poetry Northwest: [My hands reached out and plucked] and [It was so beautiful right before].

Quill Puddle: [Do you remember when], [There's a galaxy inside each blueberry], [She could have loved you], [You take another into yourself] and [That was the real thing].

The Smoking Poet: [The fish itself was water made flesh], [Heat. Sun hot on your skin], [Rain. What came pouring out], [Sometimes I remember how you with], [Meanwhile the weather went from tropical to ice], [It was the rain coming into me], [In my afternoon nap dream], [It wasn't the river coming into me] and [It begins with a glisten and then].

For Nicole

Look homeward Angel now, and melt with ruth:

CONTENTS

1.
She sang beyond the genius of the sea 1

2.
For she was the maker of the song she sang 22

3.
She measured to the hour its solitude 41

1.

She sang beyond the genius of the sea.

It begins with a glisten
metamorphosis at the core
of the language the river
speaks to itself all winter
a stronger angle of April
sun gray loess on the snow
the river eating ice from below
until comes release in a surge
of broken ice and floods the ice
dams cause. What was frozen
breaks free and the river braids
new braids and tendrils to the sea
and so becomes again the sea
drifting new icebergs toward
an old center levitated in air's
heat transubstantiated to cloud.

Salt yes. The taste of kelp permeating the skyline
and still another storm rolling in to throw more flotsam
on top of the pile the last storm left torn fishing nets
and yellow plastic buckets. It wasn't the building
swell that troubled us so much as the thought of
the thought of leaving of being forced to quit this coast
smelling of home and spilled oil and dead gulls. We could
come back couldn't we back here where we first began
to feel the ebb tide tugging our toes deep into sand?
We could maybe but it would have changed and
all the old family would have moved on or died
and then what would home be except storm swell
beach wrack ships smashed and broken open
on the reef? We left and only returned for salmon.

There is an order in the apparent chaos
of the spruce swamp but not the order
of human tragedy or love. Beneath
the snow there is horsetail tundra tea
lingonberries last year's spruce needles
four kinds of moss spruce roots and loess
mountain ground powder fine by glaciers
and years and carried here on north wind
like the rumor someone who loved you once
has died. Beneath that a lens of permafrost ice
which hasn't thawed in a million years not since
the arctic was tropical the mosquitoes sharp
enough to suck blood from a wooly mammoth.
It's thawing now in a fractal release of carbon
and more and more and soon the spruce will slump
and tumble into a new form of carbon for the air
which on second thought isn't really all that far
from the end of human love or tragedy when there is
only one left among all the dead to tell us this.

Heat. Sun hot on your skin
but the wind cool enough on
the skin not bound to the other's
skin and the afternoon cumulus
rolling in with the smell of rain
before the rain comes thunder
ozone a flash from the friction
of cloud on cloud the synapses
firing the brain on fire flaming
to orange in the frontal lobe
the tongue in circles loosening
opening wind from within you
and lips forming the word oh
and oh and if the storm kept
on storming you couldn't stand
it couldn't stay within your body
but became the body of the other
storm and too much rain rivers
overflowing the willows into
the room and through the room
filling the house and sweeping
away what you were before now
aloof inside your own skin
transparent to wind and willow
in wind leaf and sun rain
and the silence that comes after.

In the shadow I was breathing
I was breathing in the blue
snow in the shadow of birch.
I was breathing birch in blue
shadow and the birch wore snow
like a shadow like breath and more
snow was falling was breathing
shadow breathing birch the birch
was breathing my breath blue
in shadow and the moon cast
a shadow behind the breathing
snow behind the birch behind
moon the breathing was snowing
had snowed and it would snow
and the snow would gather
like a shadow of snowy birch
a shadow of blue a shadow
of breathing and my breath
rose white into blue snow.

Sometimes I remember how you with
both hands on the back of my head
pulled my tongue into you and into
you until I was drowning stroking
toward a surface still too far away to
reach in time the rippled mirror
surface of a pond into which the day's
thunderheads were infinitely descending
white curtains billowing inward in downdraft
lightning close and blue and inundation
coming but not yet not yet. Your cries in
the afternoon your cries at night after
waking you devoured me I drowned in
you we pulled each other into each
other spring then summer storms coming
you coming wet kisses I loved your smell.

Framed like this
whatever you see
becomes artifact
to what you did
not see a moment
before you came
here to stare into
the meniscus of
time's inside out.
For example this
spruce cut off from
forest by the view
and held in January
isolation daybreak
more snow now
than tree a study
in which Derrida
perfected his ideas
of erasure. Take
a priori the blue
shadowed tracks
a fox flung moments
before you looked
and having thus
leapt from potential
gaze continues her hunt
for the ever elusive
snowshoe hare. If
you'd arrived a little
later even the tracks
would have vanished

under blue snow.
Later still a portrait of
the absence of spruce.

Meanwhile the weather went from tropical to ice
and back again while species arrived and left thrived
and died mammoths camels red horses whole rainforests
buried rotted compressed by centuries into oil pumped
800 miles down the pipeline from Deadhorse to Valdez
across three mountain ranges loaded onto tankers which
mostly do not crash into Bligh Reef and spill their oil to kill
kill kill otters shearwaters puffins and deform the halibut
floated south fifty million gallons at a time refined into fuel
for all the boats and airplanes pickup trucks and snow
machines burned into gasses which rise to join other
bigger gasses from the all the burning elsewhere
trapping the sun to warm the air to melt the ice again
and so rainforest begets rainforest and new marshes form
to delight the muskrats new pools of melt water to mirror
the aurora all winter in south wind wavelets dancing
with desire glaciers longing for the still frozen days.

I'm kneeling before her devoting
myself to that place our daughter
will emerge from four months from
now now and more just above there
at the nub of the center of the center
of her whole entire self. Outside winter
but steamy and warm in here her
panties and bras my briefs and shirts
gyrating dry galaxy clusters free
from the mass of ourselves. Tongue
lips teeth the silent space between.
She's got one leg stretched high
on a washer leaning back against
the door inner thigh and the tendon
connecting her leg to herself her center
above the center gyrating in the basement
spinning until there was no building
above us and fat snowflakes fell on us
on the laundry disaster catastrophe
here at the center of the spasm
the whirl of clothes and she fell.

Rain. What came pouring out
of me wasn't the garden wasn't
the day. Wasn't refusal. Wasn't
sunset either showers building
in after heat soil and seed
convection. It wasn't the garden
springing out of me in late May
wasn't the peas' emerging green
spears. Wasn't the willing shower
falling nor the scent of wet loam.
Wasn't carrots either twin scalpel
blades forcing up tiny seeds up
to sun through the crust the last
shower formed. Wasn't seeds
nor breeze though one came up
after the rain. Maybe something
like passivity. Like the total
absorption of love's terrors
and anticipations when you wake
in the night to hail banging
the metal roof. Wasn't beauty
though beauty was there too
in broad leaves newly uncrumpled
pale photosynthesizing all the sun
they could and transmuting waves
to matter leaves like mainsails
and the future fruit radiating
messages from another shore.
But there was a moment of
transparency where nothingness
didn't awe me where time turned

to no time breeze that shower sun
each seed already encoded with spiral
forms holding the end of the seed.

When she was gone my despair was a sea
so filled with ice I slipped into it over
and over so blue-ringed I could not see
my way back to that self I was before
the fall she left. April and a cold spring
melting slow to come and more snow each night
to slow the melting more. Wishing would not bring
the sun back sooner but I thought it might
if I heaved hard enough to tilt the planet
or bring its orbit closer to the sun.
After she was gone I fell and blamed it
on the ice a shelf that had not yet begun
to melt beyond the border of the snow
crusted season into the self I know.

An opening loosening relaxing
desert turns tropic and the color
one finds inside the conch shell
once the creature has moved on
or died or been eaten and your eye
is invited inward toward the sound
the sound too of sunset wind frond
coral darkening to violet blood
a country where the eye will be dazed
concussed beyond its own internal
fluidity. Where the bursting begins
and begins and begins pulsing dewy
opening into sky beyond fuchsia
fireweed waves gulls chanting flood tide.

I want to slide into you
like a fang into a vein
a finger into the honey jar
a tongue into a mouth
want to slide into you
like a bullet into a rifle
a bee into a peony
electricity into a wire
slide into you like
an otter into underwater
a tree root into deeper
a thought into a synapse
into you like time into always
a meteorite into atmosphere
an orchid into a vase
a corpse into a coffin
like a salmon into upstream
battle into the capital city
breath into soap bubble
spruce into the stove
I want to slide into you
like a whisper into an ear
a nipple into a suck
a python into paradise

Pink essence of essence
it rose into the glass topped
pump when I pumped
the handle and into the Ford
or a five gallon bucket
in which I would scrub
grease caked parts with
a wire brush. Left too
long it would disappear
entirely transforming
to pure ether to essence
of air. I loved that smell
like nothing else bent
over the bucket scrubbing
the tiny hairs on my hands
and arms springing upright
in the evaporation. Essence
of formerly living creatures
it has life inside its scent
heady dizzy making pink
translucence volatile cool.
Ancient lives layered pressed
beneath the weight of eons
pumped up and distilled
into pink evaporating pinkness
fuel for the planet liquid
already turning to gas
pumped into everybody's
everything. It bent the world
and turned it pink when
you looked through the glass

cylinder it rose into while
I pumped as hard as I could.

In my afternoon nap dream
the mare broke into a gallop
we were bareback. The road
slid muddy and I tried to pull
her up sliding mud flying up
from her hooves but she could
not be held in by bit nor rein
at a full run now her gait sleeking
into pure speed. We'd both
run into the middle of our lives
and the gallop was a dream up
the muddy hill of the road.
I held my seat knees gripping
alongside her withers leaning
forward into wind reins tight
and her on the bit exploding
faster than she ever had
up the hill all out me clinging
to her like a seed in my dream
afternoon her running like
a mare can run only when
she knows the dream and hill.

It wasn't the river coming into me
wasn't the load of glacial silt the boils
of current the eddies shifting sandbars
driftwood gulls crying endlessly of want
the nested eagles' bickering. Wasn't salmon
either though I was there to catch them
brought my daughter there to catch them
the mountain itself concealed by cloud
then not on the exposed sandbar in a valley
the boundaries of which are disputed
by tribe and state. I held a net in the water
and hoped beyond hope a salmon would swim
in. It wasn't the glacier grinding a mountain
to powder wasn't the wind blowing mountain
into my eyes wasn't clouds by a river
large enough to create its own weather.
My daughter and I held the net together
hoping. Many salmon passed upstream
just out of reach. Wasn't the day shower
cloud the mountain emerging. Wasn't
water almost glacier which would kill us
for sure sink us to the bottom clothes
loaded with powdered mountain if we
lost our footing on the slippery rocks.
Wasn't the rocks themselves rounder
round each year with the river's silt
polishing boulders stones pebbles sand.
We could see an eagle far across the river
see water swirling upstream in eddies
while the mass of water came down
rising in the afternoon with the sun

melting the glacier faster shattering
into maelstrom whirlpool current to sweep
us away seeking fish. One king salmon swam
upstream to spawn and into our current
stretched net. We pulled her together
to shore and gutted her there saving roe
for eating and to cure for bait. Her flesh
was oily delicious beyond the others orange
beyond orange and we ate her made her us.

2.

For she was the maker of the song she sang.

It begins underground
forgotten words permafrost
said to wind before the great
congelation. Now the ice lens
contracts and birches above
slump into fresh swamp
beginning the transformation
to gas carbon from layers
of forests buried profound
and frozen all this time
bubbling forth as methane
to light the swamp eerie
autumn nights when mist
rises when fossil mammoth
bones reunite themselves
and dance again in ancient
step along the shores of risen
seas supertankers ply since an
open passage means they can.

What must the whales think
about the new water about
the clouds of krill and plankton
for supper? Baleen straining
self from the sea seismic
testing explosions trumpets
of the apocalypse reverberate
through the oil filled melon
of the beluga who loves to eat
salmon and sings more than most
who in turn is caught and eaten
by people and also sometimes
by killer whales whose dorsals
reveal their identity feeding
in pods from blubber blankets
stripped from gray whale calves
held down until the baby drowns
in the waters off Unalaska who
dive so deep to mate no human
has ever seen it hot whale love
and maybe a new calf will come
to make the migration north
in an ocean larger and a little
less salty than it was last year.

Do you remember when
we used to lie facing
each other head to hip
hungry for not nectarine
but a taste of the juices
flowing from the other
to become pure hunger
pure black cherry held by
the other's mouth where
words come from lips
tongue fricative glottal
two bent question marks
raspberry sliced cantaloupe
inverted joined moving
at the mouth the center
as if for that time we
could at last abandon
bodies and become the other
in tangerine in tongue lip
in language voice mind
and feeling plum and sun
for as long as this goes on.

There's a galaxy inside each blueberry
and blueberries carpet the tundra to every
horizon the sun sweeps around never setting
in summer's endless afternoon and mosquitoes
blacken the air each June with a hunting hum
seeking blood and more blood so they can breed
and torment the herds of caribou still migrating
ancestral paths and new paths too since it seems
everything is changing changing sunlight
by the second and minute in a cycle which has
remained mostly constant in change since
the planet achieved its tilt. Meanwhile.

She could have loved you
there on the beach weaving
toward the bluff half moon
waxing sunset and sunrise
so close together you walked
through them basalt lined
with quartz wave rounded
and the sand between each
stone. Out there moon pulled
tide onto the beach then off
it while starfish and clams
fed in the broad intertidal zone.
We could have kept going
around the bluff and on
toward Anchor Point. Otters
rode the waves in rafts
of themselves home in icy
water. A long night out
and quick morning walking
in moonlight and sunlight
down the beach and back again.
How much time do we have?
King salmon piling up at the inlets
of their home rivers hooked
blushing now ready for the season's
run in that moment of finding
after all the phosphorescent
beings beneath your separate
skins mountains and glaciers
too beautiful to live beneath.
You could die of beauty here.

I couldn't take it anymore
couldn't take white birch
screaming from the forest
at midnight white shrieks.
What could they want?
Only what I didn't have.
A future that included
birch and me walking
through and under birch
bark peeling like paper
useful as paper or for making
baskets to carry what you've
gathered what you need
blueberries desire water
for example. I couldn't
take the shrieking leaves
swelling in midnight sun
and all the birds returned
mated already or singing
out for someone someone.
Hear me now and believe
in the power of the undark
days on the trees arias
green greener the breeze
which helps them craft a note
excluding some but not all.

When the halibut gave themselves
I accepted and reeled them up
from the icy deep a hundred feet
down reeled them up from the bottom
of the bay to see their goggle eyes
staring into mine as old as mine
as many meals to admire their chocolate
and black camouflage their white
other sides. I wanted an older one
to come up to meet me here in
the boat floating atop the bay
where humpback after humpback
breached and blew beside the boat
where killer whales had killed
ten they knew of and experts talked
of this on the radio. I wanted
an older one and so I fished on
there in the boat with my father
who admired the mountains
and glaciers as much as the halibut
who came from the bottom
to meet us on the boat. I let all
but two of them go back there
to tell the story of rising against
your will into the light of pale
eyes staring back. Shearwaters
raced the boat home and they won.

You take another into yourself
and it begins a heart shaped leaf
lovevine innocent purple white
blossoms and oh how it grows
binds the railroad tracks to ties
parallel to the gleam of vanishing
binds horizon to sky more than
the erotic warblings of meadowlarks
vines into a moan in sleep in dream
green heart-shaped leaves invading
the smelt of iron and alloy and wheat
waves of wheat as far as you can see
from not a hill but a slight rise in
the prairie wind coming through
you weaving the seed heavy plain
into cello an etude in one note
and then another waves within your
body seeds transformed to toothy air
through the alchemy of yeast foam
and food opening into another's body
lovevine and innocent purple white
blossoms morning glory convulsion.

Let's say carnivorous plant.
Let's say I never want to die.
Say plethora. Say salt. Say fame.
Say cast your bottles on a hurricane
Say wheat field. Say skyscraper.
Let's say wind swaying spruce.
Say let bygones be beyonds.
Say a marigold by any other name.
Say wear your spleen on your wrist.
Let's say pretty as a puncture.
Let's say where's your pelvis?
Say roosters coming home to roost.
Let's say blue pills and pink pills.
Say kiss me like you mean it.
Say archipelago. Say verbose lagoon.
Let's say love and love and I want.
Say body politic. Say tangerine. Say
arsenic. Say lick my belly. Say it again.

That was the real thing
the first time there is
always a first time we'd
been waiting so hot for
now this tent the storm
naked raw lighting us blue
as bare as we'd ever been
sun heated air rising on
convection currents colliding
with the cool air above
into that sublime terror
the boy felt rowing toward
the night cliff in a stolen
boat. Mosquitoes blackening
the blue tent drunk on our
breath hungry for our blood
for the blood of the child
we were making in the storm
wind within wind outside
the rain's angled slash
lightning and crash coming
close wind gust leaves
ripped from the willow since
oh yes this was as real
and original as it gets naked
blue the first time making our.

Takes you at a gallop
through frosted stalks
of fireweed and grass
bent under new snow
each seed singing cling
cling as if runaway belief
could seam a torn season.
As if once past the last
cabin's smoke the trail
spurs you on north until
winter shreds her mane
and winter's burn fingers
holes in a coat you hoped
would hold some reason
to doubt her bearing. Until
the incremental shrinking
of birch and black spruce
leaves you dazed weaving
fetlock deep through boreal
forest with a horizon too
far away for the sun to see.
You could shiver a long
night here. A long night.
More snow will come.
And wind. Don't worry.

The garden gives way to winter harvest is over
and we ourselves are doomed tsunami drought
volcano melt cancer. Torpor and knowing we are
doomed do lend a certain sweetness to summer
past solstice when the angle of sun becomes
more acute when fireweed blooms from bottom
up until it turns to fluff and flies and snow
soon follows soon sanctifies what has grown
and died in encasements of white and blue dust.
If we could fix those fuchsia blossoms in honey
or jelly or wine if we could fix that color deep
in our lungs we wouldn't have to cough so with
the first inhalation of forty below. I don't know.
We are doomed to failure no matter how hard
we try to cable the continents together to launch
satellites to consume the excess carbon. If the sun
is doomed to go red and swell and devour the planet
we should suck the nectar of fireweed anyway suck
the nectar of each other again and again sun
and moon breathing and breath sweat and salt
cloud razor blue sky.

I thought I had lost her in the forest
or that she had lost me among the white spruce
the birch moonlit silver in hoarfrost
where we walked through the long night of solstice.
I stopped to listen heard nothing but wolves
howling far away madrigals to the moon.
I stopped to listen heard nothing but love
howling lost without her where has she gone.
On the nightest night of the year love is
mostly longing searching unbroken snow
for a track a sign a word in wilderness
where sleeping bears and words never go
unless your own lips wake them. Or hers do.
I wanted her to find me in the night
among the birches wanted her lips too
longed for her there under shadow and moonlight.

It was the rain coming into me
days of rain. I didn't have any
choice rain on my bald head
days of steady rain and gray
and it flowed through my body
a creature made of mostly water.
I stumbled into the forest dripping
birch and spruce cottonwood rain
on my naked head wet boots wet
to my knees in the grass in alder.
Some early mornings like this you hope
to encounter a bear and for that
encounter to go badly enough your face
ends up dangling down your chest.
Days of rain nights of rain of the steady
dripping kind running down through bald
scalp into sloshing brain through chest
and into my spine through groin
through thighs knees out through
my feet. I sloshed in boots made full
through alder through grass alone
thinking I would always from this time
forward be alone in dripping spruce
birch grass to my knees and all the planet's
water running through me through me.

Gazing up into that inverted swallow
I thrilled not at the blueblack wings
but rather the space between
the wings the absence of wings
the origin opening and opening
seizing air and not air a question
at the center of bird a warble a trill.
Who could blame me for wanting
to put my tongue there between
and between feather and down
and flesh? The sky? The sky was
a riot of blooming nasturtium and flame.

Could bears really outnumber
people there where moose emerge
from the forest like epiphanies
and vanish between birch trees
just as soon? Where spring migrations
still dim the sun with geese and cranes
and pintails and almost every other bird
one ever dreams of seeing varied thrush
brant greater yellowlegs snow bunting
long eared grebe. Everything moves!
Five species of salmon slashing upstream
to die and spawn eggs emerging from
rotting bodies like clusters of undiscovered
citrines gleaming in the gravel glaciers
in rapid retreat spruce sway earthquake
walrus slipping from thinning ice floes
into the sea where belugas and humpbacks
are still hunted and stripped of blubber
eaten to the bone inside the bone.

There came the moment when
having held you at the rim
a long time it was time to push
you over the edge of yourself
into the paroxysm that seems
to come from beyond the body
mind complex to arise from
fire and gleam unbroken snow
seems to arise from the belly
of the grazing mare from grass
but instead was breathed in
and held expelled as cirrus
wisping across an otherwise
clarified sky. July. Fireweed
in fuchsia gush pushing outward
a maximum symmetry to lure
those vanishing winged ones
who make honey who speak
in pheromones and dance
a tongue we think we understand
the beyond from which there is
no turning back a full gallop
wind lifting her mane convergence
of the old duality until you are
wholly body and that is more than
enough for now ecstasy there
and not there need in abeyance
the hum nectar the sky the sky.

The fish itself was water made flesh
silver scales striking black spots down
the back black inside the mouth hooked
teeth to seize blushing to color now she
was in the river headed upstream
through the eddies and pools through
riffles and maelstroms she was bound
for a clear creek with a gravel bed.
But our net brought her close and we
touched her our hands slipped along
her slime and we took rocks and beat
her on the head to stun her then slit
her open and the roe spilled out twin
sacks the color of sliced tangerine
full of thousands of potential kings.
She was the river the ocean the river
made solid and I slit her from anus
to throat I cut around her arterial
gills and pulled her heart out still
beating. Her flesh oily the pale flame
of her twin skeins of roe. Oh she
never made it upstream and her body
became our bodies charred and oily
from the fire. We ate her skin her
flesh. We sucked the bones clean.

3.

She measured to the hour its solitude.

It begins and glaciers free
the ice worms in semiotic
retreat revealing a mountain
not yet locked in name new
granites to parable a canyon
between used to and will be.
The river roars louder the hotter
the air these white July nights
forcing red salmon to fight
harder each spawn slashing
new eddies a thousand miles
upstream to unload their cargo
into gravel nests and die fry
emerging from underneath
the rotting parents' carcasses
all eyes and tail and mouth
ancient papyrus released into
the current one phoneme at a time.

I pull her back to me now.
She died with no word she's
becoming earth she died.
I pull her back to me now
her flesh her touch the way
she sank down around me
the way I sank into her forever.
We couldn't get enough
sinking some days her despair
finding voice even in moans
of pleasure. When I pull her
back on top of me her breasts
now she is here I can smell her
stroke bend sway she is not
her body anymore she is not
her night hair draping over me
her hazel eyes I kept sinking
into her manipulations art
she drew with swiveling hips.
There were days she would
cook and cook for me and watch
me eat my teeth pulling her
into my mouth making her me
and since she cannot die cannot
I pull her back to me now.

It must have been wildfire flaming out
of me smoke for sure I smoked in self
defense cigarette after another against
the smoke so thick it turned the sun red
the garden otherworldly stunted turned
the unburned trees strange in the red glow.
They knew they would burn we would
flee when the wind shifted west. The black
spruce burned like gasoline like sun-baked
papyrus and the words burned too beyond
the page into speech and the smoke resinous
we smoked we both smoked so did the baby.
I couldn't see across the road most days
the wildfire raged I mean raged it was wild
fire flaming out of me spruce seeds free
from the cone exploding onto the now
fertile blackened ground fireweed fluff
to turn the burn red violet next July
morels blooming through ash in rain
through maelstrom. People and horses fled
when an unpredicted west wind whipped
flames into flames into galloping until
the fire so white hot vaporized more black
spruce more transformation more smoke
we all smoked. Fire made its own weather
its own planet it was fire snorting out of me
smoke and smoke July drought heat and heat
ancient love poems scrolls and the black
spruce and wind wanted to burn to make
more forest again from ash for fireweed
for more spruce conflagration maelstrom

wildfire leaping bulldozed fire lines
firefighters fleeing my words smoking
out the baby's cries her first words a white
smoke plume satellites saw photographed
reported the wind shifting shifting until
through the new words it was clear we'd
flee we'd all have to start all over again.

Then there were those times
you engulfed me straddled
me and rode until I was all
the way inside you until
I vanished and became your
glisten your want your rhythm
as you stroked me stroked
yourself as if the sun would
never set again and the world
would green into leaf and leaf
each bud each grass blade
and seed filled with sign.
Oh you loved to ride me
that way until I thought I was
breaking apart dissipating
into the standing waves
which arise in the straits
when current and tide and wind
boil the ocean to white foam.
You became me too molecule
by molecule and carried me
inside you after the wind after
bluestem grass and the whole wide
prairie green in wind and seed
larkspur and goldenrod waves
oysterleaf beach pea anemone.

The people came together at the farm
and there was salad from the farm
and carrots arugula goat cheese bread
wine the people walked under rain
through the pasture past the poppies
and chicken coop past the broccoli
and greenhouses bursting in rain
and cucumbers past the compost
and potatoes leeks garlic peas sweet
alyssum and borage in azure bloom
in the salad the farm feeds the people
who live here and twenty nine other
families of people. Past red cabbage
the heifer grazing beneath mountains
invisible in cloud mist rain vanishing
now though so dramatic when you can
see them above the pasture through
the gate to the yurt where they went
to eat and drink and listen to poetry.
The children played and listened
and spoke fell and were hurt crying
for their fathers who kissed the hurts
and took them outside to the pasture.
Their mothers listened to poetry
were moved by its power to transform
wordsound to music to feeling they
felt deep in their bodies the women
who planted these plants. Yes they.

My breath rose white into blue
snow and the only sound other
than my breathing was the snow.
No. The birch creaked in breeze
and the snow slanted. And the snow
struck my skull with the sound
of twigs clicking in breeze.
That was all. No. A voice rose up
not my voice not the birches'
nor the snow not the voice
of blue shadow and I heard
it not the words there were
no words and the voice was
not my voice not silence nor birch.

Making love with her was like a journey
underground tunneling beneath lilac
roots past the homes of little back beetles
deeper beneath the web of moss and spruce
root the complex system of birch roots
we haven't found a fractal for beneath
the burrows of creatures now waking
from hibernation and down to the thawing
permafrost and all the creatures it contains
held in stasis for the moment but not much
longer energy patiently awaiting its leap
back into matter her dark hair flooding
over my face her nipples inviting my tongue.

The thought of even losing you fills my mind
with winter with nights of forty below
with ice fog hoarfrost and steel shattering.
What snow there is (nothing) is all the snow
there will ever be. The thought of losing
you is black spruce charred by moonlight
dogs howling on their chains nothing fusing
nothing into an icy thought you meant to write
down once but then forgot. Even losing you.
We've been losing the sun for three months now
and soon we'll lose it altogether. Winter
will begin again (losing you) when spruce cast blue
nets of shadows across (nothing) the snow
drifting the same bare place that is not there.

There were those times
she was infinite insatiable
as if flesh and flesh could
never be enough. She needed
honeysuckle cantaloupe
peonies sweet peas carrots
lilacs new potatoes radishes
and the rain mud between
the rows mud to roll around
in in mid-July and the moon
nearly full mud to coat
ourselves in to carry inside
each other. The whole garden
to consume to make part
of ourselves one molecule
at a time infinite and seasonal
asparagus later tomatoes.
I did my best to fill her up.
But she was leaving and we
both knew why she had to
leave and it made us sad
inside each other green
onions basil thyme tarragon
and the spaces in between
bean rows and sweet corn
where we filled each other
with each other with mud
sunflowers the strawberries
I would eat alone weeping in
the garden when she was gone.

Was it the ocean flowing out of me
foam and wave flooding in ebbing
the scarlet jellies drifting a life
as if destination mattered not at all
flooding ebbing pulled by what gravity
the moon generates quick razor clams
revealing themselves with a telltale hole?
Ocean pulled by predictable moon
tides but rising now licking at the beach.
It always wanted a glass surface
full of cirrus and pulling the pier
and the boats moored there low
and steep at the ebb. I was filled
with wave and need came flooding
out in a story that wanted telling
but to who to who? The animate
ocean didn't care and I felt it
felt happy to be rising growing
thinning the old ice floes to let
ancient densities discover again
the freedom of moment of drifting
south the ecstasy of dissipation.
I yearned for whaledom herring
caught in our bubble net and us
rising with mouths open wide
enough to devour a skiff to fill
ourselves with oily fish. It was
the ocean flooding out of me
squid and octopus salmon halibut
and ancient flame orange rockfish
delicious and much to be desired.

Love and its changeful unchanging
a loosening at flood the reversals.
I needed salt and the story came
foaming out to the strict meter
of water and moon and night wind.

Her nipples spoke to me only to me
said come here and suck come here
and be whole again as you were
then trailing clouds of glory trailing
clouds before language took its hold.
Her nipples spoke to me only me
they spoke to everyone and their
voices were husky and more red
dark now the daughter had fed
there. I came and sucked too and two
lines ran straight to her center
where the story began one morning
when the sun honed new edges
on everything outside honed clarity.
I sucked and they spoke to me only
to me daughter full and sleeping
they spoke to everyone and the story
they told was long and sad and sweet.

My hands reached out and plucked
the blueberries from their tiny bushes
on the tundra we were on the tundra
picking blueberries my daughter and
me we picked and we picked while
the sun cut a sharper angle across south
now it was August. My hands reached
out my fingers twirled each blueberry
from its stem my hands filled and emptied
into my bucket and so did hers child
filling her own bucket now. The sun
broke through scattered shower raindrops
sliver and slow against storm cloud sun
shower and the tundra pulled me in
pulled me closer now beyond the berries
beaming in shortwave frequencies
violet indigo cerulean azure the cloud
the whole tundra beamed back and pulled
me into it moss and lichen miniature
alder willow birch beaming back fall
in every frequency my eyes could see
and some they couldn't crimson arterial
cream chameleon chartreuse sunshower
blueberries filling our hands our buckets
our tongues our mouths pulled me into
tundra tiny and tinier. I stood up to see
and the horizon whirled until the mountain
fixed it the glacier fixed it and I knew which
direction was which. My hands reached out
and lifted my daughter across the swampy
crossing lifted her across onto the tundra

our hands reached out our fingers we filled
our buckets we knelt on the tundra our hands
reached out filling and slept there that night
the wind blew the moon rose we slept full
and when she woke she told me she dreamed
of her mare there on the tundra with her.

When we slid together time
was still time. Who could
have known that? A room
full of windows and white
curtains billowing in breeze
evening sun slanting in.
We slid together and our
hands were together tongues
nipples. You could be
disappeared in a person
like that and we were
evening still light enough
to see the sliding to know
this was the best we could
would ever become loosing
time time to undulation to
wet and glide and tongue
to tongue deep breathing
molecules of you and her
and what the wind blew
through the open windows
I don't know. Time sliding.
Belly and belly and billow.

Smoke so black I couldn't see
across the wild flame on flame
wild conflagrations black words
July heat the black spruce wild
as hot gasoline wild to flame to
spread the black seeds. I walked
out into nothing but the red ball
of sun through spruce smoke
a word someone said once
that set the lungs to wild flame
spruce flame resinous in heat.
There was nothing to breathe
except smoke and the words
you meant to say heat flame
wild smoke soaring like a cloud
the flame made of black spruce.
When the land and sky are seen
through black spruce smoke
flame and red sun words
sear the seer and the seen.

It was so beautiful right before
the end the storm moving out
clouds blown north wisping
dissolving devolving mist
in the wind faster than they
had ever maybe and then sun
days of brilliance delphinium
waist high but not in bloom
yet violet azure and poison
enough to kill a child sweet
peas too crimson fuchsia
pink and deadly. The North Pole
they predicted would be ice
free this year and nations
rushed to drop flags from submarines.
It was beautiful. I can't say how
cobalt the sky after the storm
blew out fast. Polar bears
hunting inland now walrus
crushing each other in panicked
rushes from the beach. She
rode the mare bareback to graze
the grass lush as mare's dreams
bluebells wild roses. The storm
overfilled the rain barrels and
the mountains gleamed snow
capped under between fleeing
clouds delphinium azure deeper
blue than the sky after the storm
before the end so beautiful there.

It begins with a glisten and then
it isn't about language anymore
but about that place beyond which
words become moan and sigh
and sibilant shriek a loosening
a blossoming into July nasturtium
flame and flame and the circles
a tongue can make at the center
of a person belly deep and starved
for waves night ocean the tide
coming in. You know what current
it means to melt out of yourself
and into another. What it means
beyond language hidden until
now within the double helix
within the first word the child
learns book a blossoming back
into story into the thawed pond's
mirror surface opening a self more
beautiful than yourself tide
coming in receding pools full
of tiny silver fish and mussel
shells sharp enough to cut
to the nerve iridescent in sun
circles within circles opening
the room into which you come.

www.ingramcontent.com/pod-product-compliance
Lightning Source LLC
LaVergne TN
LVHW011430080426
835512LV00005B/360